The World's Best Lawyer Jokes

In this series:

The World's Best Dirty Jokes
More of the World's Best Dirty Jokes
Still More of the World's Best Dirty Jokes
The World's Best Irish Jokes
More of the World's Best Irish Jokes
The World's Best Jewish Jokes
More of the World's Best Jewish Jokes
The World's Best Doctor Jokes
More of the World's Best Doctor Jokes
The World's Best Dirty Stories
The World's Best Dirty Limericks
The World's Best Dirty Songs
The World's Best Aussie Jokes
The World's Best Catholic Jokes
The World's Best Mother-In-Law Jokes
The World's Best Russian Jokes
The World's Best Fishing Jokes
The World's Best Salesman Jokes
The World's Best Computer Jokes
The World's Best Scottish Jokes
The World's Best Cricket Jokes
The World's Best Golf Jokes
The World's Best Maggie Thatcher Jokes
The World's Best Lawyer Jokes

The World's Best Lawyer Jokes

Edward Phillips

Illustrated by Tony Blundell

ANGUS
& ROBERTSON
PUBLISHERS

ANGUS & ROBERTSON PUBLISHERS

16 Golden Square, London W1R 4BN,
United Kingdom, and
Unit 4, Eden Park, 31 Waterloo Road,
North Ryde, NSW, Australia 2113

First published in the United Kingdom by
Angus & Robertson (UK) in 1989
First published in Australia by
Angus & Robertson Publishers in 1989

Text copyright © Edward Phillips, 1989
Illustrations © Tony Blundell, 1989

British Library Cataloguing in Publication Data
Phillips, Edward
    The world's best lawyers' jokes
    I. Title II. Blundell, Tony
    828'.91402

ISBN 0 207 16228 X

Typeset in Great Britain by New Faces, Bedford
Printed in Great Britain by Hazell Watson & Viney Limited, Aylesbury

Permission to quote the following work
is gratefully acknowledged:

page nos. 74-76
From "A Policeman's Lot" by Superintendent G A Harris,
published by Police Review Publishing Co Ltd,
14 Cross Street, London EC1N 8FE

and page nos. 77, 79
From "White Tie Tales" by John H Morecroft,
published by Bailey Bros & Swinfen Ltd,
Warner House, Folkestone, Kent CT19 6PH

A lawyer had just won a case on behalf of a client who had sued his employers for negligence after falling down a disused lift shaft. When the client was presented with the bill, he was furious.

'You've taken over two-thirds of my damages!' he stormed. 'How do you justify that?'

'Because,' said the lawyer, 'I provided the skill, the knowledge and the legal expertise to win the case.'

'But I provided the case itself,' protested the client.

'Oh, that,' scoffed the lawyer. 'Anybody can fall down a lift shaft.'

In a case of estrangement, a lawyer acting for the wife asked his client to come and see him in his office.

'Well, Mrs Robinson,' he said, 'I have finally arrived at a settlement with your husband which I feel is eminently fair to both of you.'

'Fair to both of us!' said the wife indignantly. 'I could have done that myself! Why do you think I hired a lawyer?'

An elderly actor in the classical tradition was appearing as a witness in a court case. He took the stand and swore the oath, and then the prosecuting lawyer began his cross-examination. 'What is your name?' he asked.

'Melton Mowbray,' declared the actor in ringing tones.

'And what is your occupation?'

'I am the world's greatest living actor,' was the dramatic

reply. This caused quite a stir in court, and when the case had been concluded, counsel for the defence buttonholed the old actor outside the courtroom and said, 'That was an extraordinary thing you said in the witness box. It cast doubt on all your evidence and did my client no good at all. Why on earth did you say a thing like that?'

'I had to, dear boy,' said the elderly thespian. 'Remember, I was under oath.'

A young law student was in the habit of writing passionate love letters to his girlfriend in which he swore undying devotion and promised her the earth. Suddenly the love letters ceased and, in despair, the girl telephoned the young man and said tearfully, 'Why don't you write to me any more? Is it all off between us?'

'It's not that,' said the budding lawyer. 'It's just that we're studying breach of promise cases this month.'

Counsel: 'And what happened after the accused gave you a punch on the jaw?'
Witness: 'He gave me a third one.'
Counsel: 'You mean he gave you a second one.'
Witness: 'No – I gave him the second one.'

Counsel: 'Now you understand, don't you, that you have sworn to tell the truth, the whole truth, and nothing but the truth?'
Witness: 'Well, I'll do my best, but I think I ought to tell you that I'm an estate agent by profession.'

The barrister had risen to dazzling heights of eloquence in defence of his client. 'One moment, Mr Kenwood,' interrupted the judge. 'I don't quite understand. You are protesting your client's innocence but he has already pleaded guilty.'

'I know that, my lord,' declared the barrister, 'but you and I know better than to believe a single word a man with his criminal record has to say.'

Counsel for the defence was obviously no stranger to the bottle. Red-faced and perspiring, with his bloated nose shining like a beacon, he attempted to make his point by addressing the judge thus: 'Now, m'lud, suppose I were to see you going into a public house ...'

'You mean *coming* in, don't you?' said the judge sarcastically.

'Now how can you be sure that the missing ducks were your ducks?' asked the counsel for the defence.

'Of course they were mine,' said the plaintiff, an old farmer. He then went on to describe the ducks in some detail. When he had finished, defence counsel said, 'Oh, come now, those are very common ducks. I've got some just like that in my own back yard.'

'Very likely,' said the old farmer. 'They're not the only ducks I've had stolen lately.'

Irish defence counsel in a paternity suit: 'And in conclusion, my client emphatically denies that he is the father of the twins – or, indeed, of either one of them.'

A lawyer was showing a friend around his garden of which he was justly proud. The friend noticed that the herbaceous borders were almost entirely filled with the pretty little plant known as honesty. 'I thought you'd be impressed,' said the lawyer. 'There's an old saying that honesty won't grow in a lawyer's garden. I think this completely disproves the saying!'

'On the other hand,' remarked the friend with a smile, 'it might just prove that you're no lawyer!'

After a very lengthy and tedious cross-examination, a lawyer suddenly broke off and protested to the judge, 'Your Honour, one of the jurors is asleep!'

'Well, you put him to sleep,' replied the judge, 'you wake him up!'

Irish barrister: 'It has been established that the offence was committed at half past twelve at night on the morning of the following day.'

A pickpocket visited a lawyer in his office and handed him a £100 note. 'This is a retainer,' he said. 'I want you to take my case. A chap's taking me to court for stealing his wallet. Claims he felt my hand in his pocket. I've been a pickpocket for twenty-five years and nobody ever felt my hand in his pocket.' The lawer pocketed the £100 note and agreed to take the case. When his client had gone, he felt in his pocket for the note. It had disappeared. He searched through all his pockets in vain, and just at that moment, his client walked in through the door.

'Here's your £100 note,' he said. 'I told you I was framed. I just wanted to be sure you believed me, and here's the proof.'

A lawyer's wife became fed up with her brilliant husband who always seemed so sure of himself on points of law. One afternoon, when their grandfather clock had just struck one she said, 'If I were to smash that clock to pieces with a hammer, could I be charged with killing time?'

'Oh, no,' said her husband. 'It would be a case of self-defence – the clock struck first.'

A young lawyer joined his father's firm and the old man decided to turn over part of his practice to his son. A few weeks later, the young man burst into his father's office, full of smiles and said, 'Guess what! I've just settled that Macmillan case that we've been working on for the last twenty years!'

'You've done what?' exclaimed the father. 'You idiot! I gave you that case as an annuity!'

A rich businessman was involved in a lawsuit which dragged on and on for years. Finally he went round to see his lawyer and said, 'Look here, this thing has gone on too long. I'm tired of the whole business and I want to settle.'

'Settle!' cried the lawyer. 'Oh, no! I'm determined to fight this case down to your last penny!'

When asked to explain the difference between an ordinary citizen and a lawyer, a well-known barrister explained, 'If an ordinary citizen gave you an orange, he would say, "I give you this orange." But if a lawyer gave you an orange, he would say, "I hereby give, grant and convey to you all my interest, right, title, and claim of and in this orange, together with all its rind, skin, juice, pulp and pips, and all right and advantage therein with full power to bite, cut, suck, or otherwise eat or consume the said orange, or give away or dispose of to any third party the said orange, with or without its rind, skin, juice, pulp or pips, subject to any amendments subsequently introduced or drawn up to this agreement."'

A woman was suing her neighbour for slander and defamation of character. Under cross-examination, her counsel asked her to tell the court exactly what words the neighbour had used. 'Oh, I couldn't do that, sir,' protested the woman. 'The things she said weren't fit for any decent person to hear.'

'All right,' said counsel. 'Just come over here and whisper them to the judge.'

A man who had been hurt in a motor accident spent several weeks in hospital. After his release, he was hobbling along the street on crutches when he met an old friend. 'Hello, Jim!' said the friend. 'Glad to see you up and about again. How long will it be before you can get rid of those crutches?'

'Well,' said Jim, 'my doctor says I can get along without them now, but my lawyer says I can't.'

Counsel for the defence was being particularly scathing. 'Now you claim,' he said to the plaintiff, 'that you were struck by a Range Rover, but your evidence is very confused and muddled. Are you sure it was a Range Rover or something resembling a Range Rover?'

'It resembled one all right,' said the plaintiff grimly. 'In fact, I was forcibly struck by the resemblance.'

In a case in a Dublin court, defence counsel claimed that the accused was not drunk but merely in a state of great excitement. In support he called the accused's doctor to the witness stand and asked him, 'Is it not true that the accused has a very excitable nature – have you, in fact, seen him on other occasions when he was highly excited?'

'Oh, indeed I have,' replied the doctor, 'frequently – even when sober.'

A man accused of fraud approached his counsel during a recess and demanded that another lawyer be provided to work with him. 'But why?' asked the barrister. 'Aren't you satisfied with the way I'm handling the case?'

'Yes,' said the accused. 'But the other side's got two lawyers. When one of them is talking, the other's sitting there and thinking. When you're talking, there isn't anyone doing any thinking.'

A farm labourer accused of stealing a wheelbarrow protested his innocence in court. In examination, prosecuting counsel said, 'You say you are innocent, yet you have heard the evidence of two witnesses who swear that they saw you take the wheelbarrow.'

'That's nothing,' scoffed the accused. 'I can produce a dozen witnesses who will swear that they didn't see me take it.'

A tradesman who was unable to obtain payment of a bill consulted a lawyer. 'Now you say this man owes you a considerable sum,' said the lawyer. 'What did he say when you presented your bill?'

'He told me to go to the devil,' replied the tradesman. 'And so I came round to you.'

A woman visited her family solicitor and said, 'I'd like to go over my will again, Mr Jenks. I'm a bit worried about ...'

'Don't you worry about a thing, Mrs Smith,' said the solicitor, 'just leave it all to me.'

'I suppose I might as well,' said Mrs Smith with a sigh. 'You'll get it all in the end.'

A well-known lawyer commissioned a portrait in oils and was very pleased with the result. The painting showed him in a casual pose with one hand in his pocket. A friend remarked that it would have been much more realistic if it had showed him with his hand in someone else's pocket.

It has been said that Moses was a great lawgiver but the fact that he limited himself to only ten commandments and kept them short and easy to understand shows that he was no lawyer.

An elderly and very learned judge ruled against a young barrister on a point of law. The young lawyer so far forgot himself as to say loudly, 'My lord, I am amazed!' His leader, a senior barrister, hurriedly rose to his feet. 'My lord, I must apologise for my young friend's hasty and unconsidered

remark. When he is as old as I am, he will not be amazed at anything your lordship says.'

'You seem to be in some distress,' said the kindly judge to the witness. 'Is anything the matter?'

'Well, your Honour,' said the witness, 'I swore to tell the truth and nothing but the truth, but every time I try, some lawyer objects.'

At an important trial, a judge consistently ignored plaintiff's counsel. Despite the barrister's continued protests that he represented the plaintiff, the judge took no notice other than to instruct counsel to sit down. At last, counsel could stand it no longer. He jumped to his feet and shouted, 'My lord, I represent the plaintiff and I am trying to do the best I can for my client.'

'Exactly,' said the judge. 'That's why I keep telling you to sit down.'

Counsel: 'Now were you or were you not bitten on the premises?'
Witness: 'Well, anatomy's not my strong point, sir, but I'll tell you this – I couldn't sit down for a week!'

A very successful and elderly barrister was sitting at the breakfast table reading the *Law Review*. His wife sat opposite him in silence, just as she had done every morning for the last thirty years. Thinking to break the boredom, she suddenly said, 'Anything interesting in the *Law Review* this morning, dear?'

Without looking up, the barrister grunted, 'Don't be silly, dear.'

'You are charged,' said counsel for the prosecution, 'with feloniously and with malice aforethought appropriating to your own use a motorised vehicle the property of Henry Williams of 43 Denman Street, on or about the 8th of July of this year, and of unlawfully conveying said vehicle from the premises without the owner's permission or consent. How do you plead to this charge?'

'Not guilty,' said the prisoner. 'All I did was steal a car.'

A social worker was visiting a prisoner and in the course of conversation asked him what he had been charged with. 'Stealing a wristwatch,' said the prisoner. 'It was a very valuable watch – worth more than £1000. I had the best lawyer I could afford. He made out a strong case and proved that I had a watertight alibi, supported by six witnesses. His speech to the jury was brilliant, but it didn't do any good – I got three months.'

'I don't understand why you weren't acquitted,' said the social worker.

'Well, there was one weak spot in my defence,' said the prisoner. 'They found the watch in my pocket.'

An old juryman was being sworn in. 'Speak up!' he said to the clerk of the court. 'I can't hear what you're saying.'

'Are you deaf?' asked the judge.

'Yes, my lord – I'm deaf in one ear.'

Counsel for the defence jumped to his feet. 'My lord, I request that this man be excused. It is essential that jurymen should hear both sides.'

First lawyer: 'My lord, despite the fact that my learned friend for the defence is an unmitigated scoundrel ...'

Second lawyer: 'My lord, we all know that my learned friend for the prosecution is a notorious liar ...'

Judge: 'Counsel will kindly confine their remarks to such matters as are in dispute.'

At a cocktail party, a lawyer was trying to obtain some free medical advice from a doctor. 'Tell me, doctor,' he said, 'which side is it best to lie on?'

'The side that pays you the biggest retainer,' replied the doctor.

Two men were walking through a cemetery. They stopped before a tombstone which bore the following inscription: 'Here lies a lawyer and an honest man.' One turned to the other and said, 'You wouldn't think there'd be room for two men in such a small grave.'

Irish barrister: 'Were you in the vicinity of the accused when he committed the crime?'
Irish witness: 'No, sir – but I was standing next to him.'

Barrister addressing the jury: 'The only failing which the prisoner has is that of relying on thieves and rogues of the worst kind. Gentlemen of the jury, the unhappy man in the dock puts implicit faith in you.'

The widow was in a complaining mood. 'Don't talk to me about lawyers!' she confided to a friend. 'I've had so much trouble settling my late husband's estate, sometimes I wish he'd never died!'

A lawyer was talking to a man who had served as a juror on a number of occasions. 'Tell me,' he said, 'who has the most influence on you in court – the lawyers, the judge or the witnesses?'

'Well,' said the experienced juryman, 'I'm a plain man and I'm not influenced by the lawyers or the judge or the witnesses. I just look at the man in the dock and I say to myself, "If he's not done nothing, why is he here?" And I bring 'em all in guilty.'

A young barrister was appearing in court on a fairly hopeless case. The judge interrupted him at one point and said, 'When you can prove that two blacks make a white, I'll listen to your argument.'

'I think I can do that, my lord,' he said. 'I once knew a black cock and a black hen who produced a white egg.' The judge listened respectfully to the rest of his argument.

Two partners in a law firm were briefed for an important fraud case. One of them had to leave for a conference abroad just before the end of the trial and his partner promised to let him know the verdict as soon as it was announced. A week later, he received a telex message which simply said, 'Justice has triumphed!' He immediately sent an urgent message back which read: 'Appeal at once!'

A young man appeared as a witness in a court case. Prosecuting counsel was not at all happy with his evidence and said sharply, 'Has anyone been telling you what to say in court?'

'Yes, sir,' replied the young man. 'My father.'

'I see,' said the lawyer. 'And what exactly did he tell you?'

'He said the lawyers would try to get me all mixed up but if I stuck to the truth, I'd be all right.'

'I do wish you would pay a little attention to what I am saying to you,' said a barrister to an awkward witness.

'I'm already paying as little as I can,' said the witness.

Counsel for the complainant in a divorce case was examining his client on the stand. 'Now let me see if we have all the facts straight,' he said. 'You maintain that every night when you returned home from work, you discovered that your wife was hiding a different man in the wardrobe. Is that correct?'

'Yes, it is,' said the husband.

'And this, of course, was very upsetting to you.'

'Of course it was! I never had any room to hang up my clothes!'

A famous barrister died and many members of the legal fraternity attended his funeral. One of them was delayed and did not arrive until the minister was halfway through his sermon. As he took his seat, he whispered to his neighbour, 'Have I missed much?'

'No,' his neighbour whispered back, 'they've just opened for the defence.'

A famous barrister was once appearing in court on behalf of a lady with the unusual name of Tickle. He began his remarks by saying, 'Tickle, the defendant, my lord . . .'.

'Tickle her yourself,' interrupted the judge. 'You're nearer than I am.'

Lawyer (to flustered witness): 'Now sir, did you or did you not, on the date in question, or at any other time, say or in any way intimate to the defendant, that the defendant was or had been in any way implicated in the events which have been described to this court, or that there was any suspicion in your mind that this may have been the case, notwithstanding that the defendant was not and could not have been in the vicinity during the period that the events aforementioned took place or might have taken place, assuming that they took place at all? Answer yes or no.'

Witness: 'Yes or no what?'

A rather unsuccessful solicitor died suddenly and his friends were very surprised when his will was disclosed because he had left very few effects. 'I suppose,' said one of his acquaintances, 'it was because he had so few causes.'

A lawyer's wife was complaining to her husband one morning at breakfast. 'We need new curtains,' she said. 'The dining room suite is a disgrace, and the whole house needs redecorating.'

'Look,' said her husband, 'I'm working on a big society divorce case at the moment. As soon as I've finished breaking up their home, I'll refurnish ours.'

Judge to defendant: 'Have you a lawyer?'
Defendant: 'No, judge, I don't need one. I'm going to tell the truth.'

A lawyer died in penniless circumstances and his friends decided to get up a subscription in order to give him a decent burial. One of them approached the Lord Chief Justice, explained the situation and asked for a shilling.

'A shilling to bury a lawyer!' exclaimed the Lord Chief Justice. 'Here's a guinea – bury twenty-one of them!'

A famous attorney had just won a difficult case for a lady and she approached him after the trial and said, 'How can I ever show my appreciation for what you have done?'

'Madam,' said the great lawyer, 'ever since the Phoenicians invented money, there has been only one answer to that question.'

A man accused of stealing a watch was acquitted on insufficient evidence. Outside the courtroom he approached his lawyer and said, 'What does that mean – acquitted?'

'It means,' said his lawyer, 'that the court has found you innocent. You are free to go.'

'Does that mean I can keep the watch?' asked his client.

A man had been convicted of theft on circumstantial evidence. When the case was sent for appeal, he revealed to his lawyer that he had been in prison at the time the crime was committed. 'Good heavens, man!' said the lawyer. 'Why on earth didn't you reveal that fact at the trial?'

'Well,' said the man, 'I thought it might prejudice the jury against me!'

Counsel: 'You are charged with stealing a motor vehicle. Have you any witnesses?'

Accused: 'No. I never take along any witnesses when I commit a robbery.'

'I wonder why it is,' said a lawyer, 'that my beard has turned grey so much sooner than my hair?'

'Because,' said a friend, 'you have worked so much harder with your jaws than with your brains.'

A very powerfully-built young man was up in court charged with assault and battery. The prosecuting counsel's cross-examination was unremitting but throughout it all, the young man maintained that he had merely pushed the plaintiff 'a little bit'. 'It is not clear to the court exactly what you mean by a "a little bit",' said counsel. 'For the benefit of the jury, I want you to step down here and show us just how hard you pushed the plaintiff.'

The young man stepped down from the dock and approached counsel. When he reached him, he slapped him hard in the face, kicked him in the shins, picked him up bodily and threw him to the floor. Then he calmly turned to the jury and said, 'About one-tenth as hard as that.'

First man: 'And how do you earn a living?'
Second man: 'I don't. I'm a lawyer.'

A man was charged with a petty offence and the prosecuting counsel asked him, 'Can you produce anyone who can vouch for your good character?'

'Yes, sir,' said the man, 'the chief constable.' It so happened that the chief constable was in court that morning and he protested, 'Why, I don't even know the man!'

'There you are then,' said the accused. 'I have lived in this area for twenty-five years and if the chief constable doesn't know me, isn't that enough character for you?'

It is said that the reason most wives are opposed to divorce is that they don't like the idea of sharing their husband's money with a lawyer.

Lawyer: 'Excellent! You've got the most watertight case I've ever come across! The other fellow hasn't got a leg to stand on.'
Client: 'In that case, I don't think I'll pursue it any further. That was the other fellow's case I was giving you.'

A trial was in progress in Reykjavik, capital of Iceland, land of the midnight sun. 'Now then,' thundered counsel for the prosecution, 'Where were you on the night of December 7th to March 2nd?'

A lawyer applied to a judge for a re-trial after his client had been found guilty. 'I've uncovered important new evidence,' he said. 'What is the nature of this evidence?' asked the judge.

'Well,' said the lawyer, 'I found out this morning that my client has an extra £1000 that I didn't know about before.'

Irish barrister: 'My lord, up until now, the whole of the evidence is entirely in the dark but now the cloud of doubt begins to crack and the cat is let out of the bag!'

A prominent lawyer had overstepped the mark and was obliged to apologise to the court. He bowed to the judge and said, 'Your Honour is right and I am wrong, as your Honour generally is.' The judge is still trying to work out whether he had been complimented or insulted.

Lawyer: 'As a youngster, my greatest ambition was to be a pirate.'
Client: 'Congratulations! Not everybody achieves his boyhood ambition.'

Overbearing judge: 'Everything you say, Mr Jones, is going in at one ear and out at the other.'
Smart lawyer: 'I'm sure it is, my lord. After all, what is there to stop it?'

The famous American General, Ulysses S Grant was a very shabby dresser and of generally unprepossessing appearance. One dark wintery night, he arrived at a small tavern in Galena, Illinois. The court was in session in town and a group of lawyers was huddled around the blazing fire. One of them noticed Grant and said jokingly, 'Here's a stranger, gentlemen, and by the looks of him, I'd say he's travelled through hell itself to get here!'

'I have indeed,' replied Grant good-humouredly. The other lawyers chuckled and the one who had spoken first said, 'And how did you find things down there?'

'Much the same as here,' replied Grant with a smile, 'lawyers all closest to the fire.'

Mark Twain once said that a jury consists of twelve persons chosen to determine which side has the better lawyer.

A young lawyer was visiting his club when he noticed a distinguished judge sitting by himself drinking mineral water. Thinking to ingratiate himself, he went up to the judge and said, 'Good evening, sir. Will you allow me to buy you a drink? They do a very good cocktail here made up of equal parts of brandy, rum and vodka. Have you tried it?'

'No,' grunted the judge. 'But I've tried a lot of fellows who have.'

A notorious thief had just been acquitted on a burglary charge, thanks to the good efforts of his lawyer. Thanking the lawyer after the trial, he said, 'I'm very grateful. Perhaps I can drop in and see you some time?'

'All right,' said the lawyer, 'but make it in the daytime, will you?'

First juror: 'We shouldn't be here very long. One look at those two fellows convinces me that they're guilty.'
Second juror: 'Not so loud, you fool! That's counsel for the prosecution and counsel for the defence!'

In the old days in Ireland, no court ever sat on a Good Friday, but on one occasion a judge announced that, owing to pressure of work, he would convene the court on that day. Muttered one lawyer to another, 'If he does, he'll be the first judge who ever sat on Good Friday since Pontius Pilate.'

A very short-tempered lawyer was bullying a witness. 'I insist that you answer the question with a simple yes or no,' he shouted.

'There are some questions,' said the witness calmly, 'that cannot be answered with a simple yes or no.'

'Rubbish!' stormed the lawyer. 'Give me an example.'

'All right,' said the witness. 'Have you stopped beating your wife?'

A lady asked a lawyer what was the exact difference between a solicitor and a barrister. 'Precisely the same,' replied the lawyer, 'as that between a crocodile and an alligator.'

Judge: 'Do you have a lawyer?'
Accused: 'No.'
Judge: 'This is a serious case. Do you wish me to grant you legal aid for a lawyer?'
Accused: 'Never mind a lawyer. Just get me a couple of good witnesses.'

A very well-known lawyer was fond of displaying his knowledge of the law on any and every occasion. He was even in the habit of lecturing the office-boy on the intricacies of jurisprudence. One day, one of the office-boy's friends asked him, 'How much do they pay you at that office?' '£10,000 a year,' said the boy.

'£10,000 – for an office-boy!' said his friend, amazed.

'Yes,' said the lad. '£30 a week and the rest in legal advice.'

Prosecuting Counsel: 'Now, this man's wallet was in his inside coat pocket. He was wearing a very tight suit and it was closely buttoned. How did you manage to remove the wallet?'
Accused: 'I usually charge £250 for six lessons, sir.'

Counsel: 'Now you maintain that the man in the dock is the same man who ran into you and knocked you down with his car. Can you swear to the man?'
Witness: 'I did, but he only swore back at me and drove off.'

Counsel: 'Are you seriously trying to tell the court that your husband, whom I can only in all honesty describe as a physical wreck, gave you that black eye?'
Plaintiff: 'Well, he wasn't a physical wreck until he gave me the black eye.'

It has been said that there are seven essential requisites for going to law: a good cause, a good lawyer, good evidence, good witnesses, a good judge, a good jury, and good luck!

Counsel: 'Now you say that at this point you stood up.'
Witness: 'I said I stood. How else can you stand but up?'
Counsel: 'Thank you. You may stand down.'

A farmer was engaged in litigation against his neighbour. In conversation with his lawyer, he said, 'I know I haven't got a very strong case. How would it be if I sent the judge a couple of nice, fat ducks?'

'Don't you dare!' said the lawyer, aghast. 'That would completely ruin your chances and might lead to very serious consequences.'

The case came to court and judgement was given in favour of the farmer. The lawyer was quite surprised at the outcome and said as much to his client after the trial.

'Well, I expect it was them ducks what did it,' said the farmer with a grin.

'Good lord!' exclaimed the lawyer. 'You don't mean to say you sent them after all!'

'Yes, I did,' said the farmer, 'but I sent them in the other chap's name!'

Counsel: 'Now can you positively identify the man in the dock as the same man you saw breaking into the off-licence?'
Witness: 'Well, I think . . .'
Counsel: 'This court is not interested in what you think! We want to hear what you know!'
Witness: 'How can I tell you what I know unless I think. I can't talk without thinking – I'm not a lawyer.'

Did you hear about the very persistent young lawyer who spent a whole evening trying to break a girl's will?

A successful barrister was regaling a dinner party with stories about his early days.

'I'll never forget my very first day as a young lawyer. I had rented a small office and had a telephone installed. I was sitting there on that first morning, waiting for a client when I heard someone outside in the corridor. He rang the bell. I shouted, "Come in!" and then grabbed the telephone, intending to give the impression that I was very busy. As the man came in, I said down the phone, "Certainly, Lord Mathieson, I'll look into the matter of Value Added Tax first thing in the morning. And you can leave all the merger details to me. I had Sir Solness on the phone earlier about the mix-up over the Debenture Stock – it's pretty urgent but I think I can sandwich your case in between that and the Baldwin bankruptcy affair. Yes, all right – I'll call you back tomorrow." Confident that I had impressed my first client, I hung up and said, "Good morning – how can I help you?"

"I'm from British Telecom, mate," he said. "I've come to connect your phone."'

'Just what is a retaining fee?' a man asked a solicitor. 'Well,' said the solicitor, 'a retaining fee is the money paid to the lawyer before he will take on a case for a client.'

'Oh, I see,' said the man. 'A bit like putting money in the meter before you get any gas.'

Definition of a lawyer: a man who persuades two other men to strip for a fight and then runs off with their clothes.

Counsel: 'Have you ever been married?'
Witness: 'Yes, sir.'
Counsel: 'And whom did you marry?'
Witness: 'A woman, sir.'
Counsel: 'Yes, well, I assumed that. I never heard of anyone marrying a man.'
Witness: 'My sister did.'

A man charged with stealing a horse was acquitted after a long trial. After the trial was over, he went back to see the judge on the following day and demanded that his lawyer be arrested. 'What on earth for?' asked the judge.

'Well,' said the man, 'I didn't have enough money to pay him his fee so he went and took the horse I stole!'

An old offender listened patiently while his lawyer challenged the jurors one by one. Finally, he leaned over and whispered, 'Challenge the bloke on the bench. I've been up in front of him before and he's prejudiced against me.'

Counsel: 'Now you claim you actually saw the defendant throw the stone?'
Witness: 'Yes.'
Counsel: 'How big was the stone?'
Witness: 'I should say it was a stone of some size.'
Counsel: 'How big exactly?'
Witness: 'Fairly large.'
Counsel: 'Can't you be more precise? Can't you compare it with some other object?'
Witness: 'Well, I would say it was about as large as a lump of chalk.'

'It's worth £500 to my client,' whispered the crooked lawyer to the foreman of the jury, 'if you can manage to bring in a verdict of second degree manslaughter.'

The verdict was indeed manslaughter in the second degree and the lawyer met the juror after the trial, thanked him and paid him the money.

'It wasn't easy,' said the foreman of the jury. 'All the others wanted an acquittal.'

During a lengthy trial the judge reproved counsel for the defence for making of lot of unnecessary noise. 'I'm sorry, your Honour,' said the lawyer. 'I've lost my overcoat.'

Replied the judge, 'People often lose whole suits in here without making such a disturbance.'

'It's time you had a talk with Jimmy,' said the lawyer's wife. 'He's twelve now and there are certain things you ought to tell him – you know what I'm talking about.'

'All right, dear,' said the lawyer. 'I'll have a word with him right away.' He took his son into his study and closed the door. 'Now, Jimmy,' he said, 'it's time for us to have a man-to-man talk.'

'OK, Dad,' said Jimmy. 'What about?'

'About the alleged facts of life,' said his father.

A man consulted a lawyer about collecting a debt of £500 owed to him by a neighbour. 'Have you anything in writing to substantiate this debt?' asked the lawyer.

'No, I haven't,' said the man. 'It was a verbal agreement.'

'Then what you have to do is this,' said the lawyer. 'Write him a letter asking for immediate repayment of the £1000 he owes you.'

'But it's only £500,' protested the man.

'Exactly,' replied the lawyer. 'He'll write and tell you so and then we'll have the proof we need.'

The young lady in the witness box was a 'model' and she was revealing more and more of her assets as she crossed and recrossed her legs. Counsel for the defence suddenly jumped to his feet and said, 'Point of order, your Honour. I've just thought of something!'

'So has every other man in this courtroom,' said the judge with a smile.

In an action for damages against the owner of a dog which had worried some sheep, defence counsel based his case on the grounds that it was, in fact, the plaintiff's own dog which had attacked the sheep.

'Now,' said counsel, 'you admit that the defendant's dog and your own are identical?'

'You couldn't tell the difference between them,' said the plaintiff.

'Since you were some distance away when the incident took place, how can you be so sure that it was the defendant's dog you saw and not your own?'

'Well, in the first place, my dog's been dead for three weeks ...'

Counsel for the defence was making his closing speech. It went on and on and on until finally the judge felt compelled to interrupt and ask that he come to a conclusion.

'I beg your pardon, my lord,' said counsel, 'but I am only acting on my client's behalf. If the verdict goes against him, he may lose his liberty for a considerable period of time. Surely I may be allowed some latitude?'

'It's not the latitude I'm complaining about,' said the judge. 'It's the longitude.'

Counsel: 'Now will you please tell the court why you didn't help the defendant in the fight?'
Witness: 'I didn't know which one was going to be the defendant, did I?'

Counsel: 'Have you followed me so far, my lord?'
Judge: 'Indeed I have, Mr Chambers, for the last hour and a half, and if I thought I could find my way back alone, I'd go back now.'

Counsel: 'Now for the last time, do you plead guilty or not guilty?'
Accused: 'How do I know until I've heard the evidence?'

A man was anxious to find out what profession his young son would take up so he left him in his room with a Bible, an apple and a £5 note. If he returned and found him reading the Bible, he would put him into the Church. If he was eating the apple, he would make a farmer of him. And if he was more interested in the £5 note, he would put him into finance or banking. When he finally opened the door, he found his son sitting on the Bible, eating the apple and with the £5 note in his pocket. 'That settles it!' he said. 'The boy's a born lawyer!'

Counsel: 'Now is it true that this is the fifth person you've knocked down this year?'
Accused: 'No, sir. One of them was the same person twice.'

A lawyer explaining to a jury the difference between presumptive and circumstantial evidence said, 'If you see a man going into a public house, that is presumptive evidence. If you see him coming out of a public house wiping his mouth, that is circumstantial evidence.'

Lawyer: 'Now where exactly did the man kiss you?'
Witness: 'On the mouth, sir.'
Lawyer: 'No, no – I mean where were you at the time?'
Witness: 'In his arms, sir.'

A burglar asked the lawyer who was defending him, 'How long do you think this business is going to last?'

'Well,' said the lawyer, 'for me about three hours. For you, I should think about three years.'

Counsel: 'Did you see the prisoner at the bar?'

Witness: 'No, sir. He was lying on his back in the street when I got to the pub.'

Irish barrister: 'Do you know what an alibi is?'

Irish defendant: 'Yes, your Honour – it's being in two places at the same time.'

A man charged with forgery protested that he couldn't even write his own name. 'Ah,' said counsel for the prosecution, 'but you're not charged with writing your own name!'

Counsel: 'And just how far were you from the accident when it took place?'
Witness: 'Seventeen feet, four and a half inches.'
Counsel: 'Oh, come now! How can you be so exact?'
Witness: 'I knew some damn fool would ask me so I measured it.'

Irish barrister defending a man accused of returning a borrowed lawnmower in a damaged condition: 'My lord, I intend to prove my client's innocence in three ways. First I intend to show that he never borrowed the lawnmower in the first place. Secondly, I will show that the lawnmower was already damaged when he borrowed it. And thirdly, I will prove that it was in perfect condition when he returned it.'

Lawyer: 'If you want my honest opinion ...'
Client: 'I don't want your honest opinion – I want your professional advice.'

A lawyer has been defined as a man who helps you get what's coming to him.

The wall between Heaven and Hell was in a poor state and badly in need of repair. St Peter asked the Devil to pay half the costs of the renovations but the Devil refused point blank to contribute a penny.

'But we have an agreement,' protested St Peter. 'If you don't pay your share, I shall sue.'

'Oh yes?' said the Devil. 'And where are you going to find a lawyer?'

A barrister was defending a man accused of breaking and entering. In his speech for the defence, he said, 'My lord, it is our contention that the defendant did not, in fact, break into the house. He found the dining room window standing open and he inserted his arm and removed a few articles from the sideboard. Since his arm – in this case his right arm – is only a part of his body, there are no grounds for punishing the whole individual for the action of one of his limbs.'

'The argument has some merit,' said the judge. 'Accordingly, I sentence the defendant's right arm to eighteen months imprisonment. He may accompany it or not, as he pleases.'

The barrister and the defendant smiled at each other. Then the defendant unscrewed his artificial arm, placed it on the bench, and walked out.

Counsel: 'What made you wait eighteen months before suing Mr Jones for calling you a hippopotamus?'

Witness: 'I didn't know what a hippopotamus looked like until I went to the zoo yesterday.'

A minister, a doctor and a lawyer hired a boat in order to indulge in a little fishing. The weather worsened and the boat began to drift dangerously out to sea. The lawyer volunteered to swim ashore to get help. The minister said a prayer for his safety and the lawyer jumped overboard and began to swim ashore. After a few minutes, the others were horrified to see a large killer shark swimming towards him. Nearer and nearer it came but then, at the last moment, it veered off and swam away.

'It's a good job I said that prayer for him,' remarked the minister with relief.

'I don't think that had anything to do with it,' said the doctor. 'I believe it was just professional courtesy.'

Counsel: 'Do you fully understand the nature of the charge which has been brought against you? You are accused of breaking and entering – and not only did you take all the money you could find in the house, you also took a large quantity of very valuable jewellery.'

Client: 'Yes, well, my old mother used to say that money alone does not bring happiness.'

Prosecuting counsel became fed up with the judge's continually ruling against him, and at last, he collected his papers together and began to leave the court. 'Mr Stevens,' said the judge, 'are you trying to show your contempt for this court?'

'No, your Honour,' replied the barrister. 'I am trying to conceal it.'

Counsel: 'You say that you haven't spoken to your wife for ten years? How do you explain that?'
Witness: 'I didn't like to interrupt her.'

Prosecuting counsel: 'You are charged with knocking the plaintiff down in the street and robbing him of all his possessions except his gold watch, a charge to which you have pleaded guilty.'
Accused: 'You mean he had a gold watch with him at the time?'
Prosecuting counsel: 'He had.'
Accused: 'Then I'd like to change my plea to guilty but insane.'

Medical authorities claim that it is safer to sleep on the right side only. They claim that it is dangerous to the health to lie on both sides, but it doesn't seem to do lawyers any harm.

Counsel for the defence was half-way through his summing-up when he noticed that one of the jurymen was sound asleep. 'My lord,' he said indignantly, 'I must protest! One of the jurors is asleep!'

'Well, wake him up,' said the judge. Counsel crossed to the jury box and roughly shook the man awake. 'How long have you been asleep?' he demanded.

'I don't know,' replied the juror. 'How long have you been talking?'

A young barrister got into terrible difficulties while conducting his first case and the kindly old judge intervened on several occasions. Finally, addressing opposing counsel, he said, 'I hope you don't mind, Mr Hyde-White – I am merely trying to give our young friend some ideas.'

'I shouldn't bother, my lord,' repled Mr Hyde-White, acidly. 'He's got no place to put them.'

A man who was accused of stealing a set of golf clubs was acquitted thanks to the services of a very clever lawyer. When he received his bill, he rang the lawyer and said, 'I know that £500 is quite a reasonable fee for your services but I'm afraid I can't lay my hands on that amount just at the moment. Would you settle for a brand new set of golf clubs?'

He saw a lawyer killing a viper
  On a dunghill by his own stable;
And the Devil laughed, for it put him in mind
  Of Cain, and his brother Abel.

– Coleridge

A very vain and overbearing barrister caused a great deal of amusement in court when his wig became disarranged. Unable to appreciate the joke, he appealed to the judge. 'My lord,' he said, 'do you see anything ridiculous in my wig?'

'Only your head,' replied the judge.

Counsel: 'Now do you understand the nature of an oath?'
Witness: 'I should do. I was in the car that bumped into yours at the traffic lights this morning.'

A lawyer challenged a juror who appeared in every way to be a thoroughly respectable and solid citizen. 'On what grounds is the challenge based?' asked the judge.

'On the grounds,' replied the lawyer, 'that he looks to be the sort of man who would be unduly influenced by the evidence.'

Although barristers generally show a proper respect for judges, they can at times be very scathing. One elderly counsel, on being asked by a judge on what authority he based a certain point of law, replied, 'Usher, go into the library and bring me any elementary text-book on Common Law.'

Counsel: 'Now is it true that for many years you have kept your wife under complete subjection and control?'
Witness: 'Yes, sir. I'm sorry but you see ...'
Counsel: 'Oh, don't bother to apologise. Just tell me how you do it.'

An elderly gentleman sent for his lawyer in order to draw up his will. 'I want to leave all my stocks and bonds to my eldest son, John,' he said.

'Don't do that,' said the lawyer. 'Leave them to David – he'll make much better use of them.'

'All right,' said the old man. 'Then I want to leave my company to my daughter, Mary.'

'Leave it to John,' said the lawyer. 'Mary knows nothing about business.'

'John it is then. I'll leave the house and grounds to Mary.'

'Better leave them to Jane. Mary's quite well off in her own right and ...'

'Look here,' interrupted the old man, 'who's dying – you or me?'

A man showed a lawyer a £20 note and asked him whether, in his opinion, it was genuine. The lawyer examined the note and said, 'This seems perfectly genuine to me.' He then placed the note in his wallet and continued, 'My minimum fee for advice is £25 so if you would just let me have your cheque for £5, that will finalise the matter.'

Counsel for the defence had been on his feet for three hours and when his closing address finally ended, his opponent, a hardened old veteran, rose to his feet and said, 'My lord, I will follow the example of my learned friend and submit my case without argument.'

A man visited a lawyer in his office and asked him to act in his defence in an impending lawsuit. He outlined the facts of the case and when he had finished, the lawyer demanded an assurance that everything he had been told was the truth. 'Oh, yes,' his client replied, 'I thought it best to tell you the truth and let you put in the lies yourself.'

The judge was over half an hour late in arriving at court. He apologised for keeping everybody waiting and explained that he had got a splinter in his finger.

A young barrister was heard to mutter to his senior, 'The old fool's been scratching his head!'

The witness was a beautiful blonde with big blue eyes. Counsel for the prosecution asked sternly, 'Now where were you on the night of Monday last?'

'I was having dinner with ... a friend,' she replied demurely.

'And Tuesday?' counsel continued. 'I was having dinner with ... another friend,' was the reply. Counsel leaned forward and lowered his voice. 'And what are you doing tonight?' he murmured.

Counsel for the defence jumped to his feet. 'I object!' he cried. 'On what grounds?' said the judge. 'on the grounds that I asked her first!' he replied.

There are two kinds of lawyers: those who know the law and those who know the judge.

A very absent-minded barrister had been engaged to defend a man accused of fraud. Forgetting for the moment which side he was representing, he rose to his feet and said, 'Gentlemen of the jury, the man before you has the reputation of being one of the biggest rogues and liars in the City.'

There was a stir in the court and junior counsel tugged at his senior's sleeve and whispered urgently, 'We're appearing for the defence, sir!' Without batting an eyelid, the barrister

continued, 'But, gentlemen of the jury, what great and good man has ever lived who was not slandered by his contemporaries?'

'I don't care to speak ill of any man behind his back, gentlemen, but I believe the man who has just left the room is a solicitor.

– Samuel Johnson

A claim was being made against a road haulage company for the loss of twenty-four pigs which had died in transit through negligence. 'My client has suffered a great loss,' said counsel for the plaintiff. 'This is not just a case of the loss of one or two pigs – but of twenty-four pigs! Twenty-four! Twice as many, gentlemen of the jury, as there are of you in that box!'

Lawyer, reassuring his client just before going into court: 'Now keep calm and don't lose your head. Just tell the jury, in my own words, exactly what happened.'

A man called in to see a solicitor to enlist his help in filling out a passport application. When the solicitor came to endorse the passport photograph, he absent-mindedly wrote, 'I certify that this is a true likeness of the accused.'

'Do you have a criminal lawyer in this town?'
'Well, we're pretty sure we do but we haven't been able to prove it yet.'

Counsel for the defence lost his temper with counsel for the prosecution and shouted, 'You are the biggest fool I've ever set eyes on!'

'Order, order!' said the judge sternly. 'You seem to forget that I am in the room.'

Counsel: 'Now you say you met the man at ten minutes past nine?'
Witness: 'Yes.'
Counsel: 'On a lonely country road, with no clocks about, on a dark, moonless night?'
Witness: 'Yes.'
Counsel: 'And yet you claim you remember that it was precisely ten minutes past nine! Did you speak to the man?'
Witness: 'Yes.'
Counsel: 'What did you say to him?'
Witness: 'I said, "Please can you tell me the time?"'

Counsel for the defence: 'You, sir, are an incompetent rogue, and before this case is over, I shall have the pleasure of showing you up for the bumbling idiot you are!'
Counsel for the prosecution: 'And you, sir, are a cheat and a liar, and know as much about the law as a child of five!'
Judge: 'Now that learned counsel have identified each other, let the case proceed.'

A lawyer was called to account by his colleagues for taking less than the usual fee from a client, thus undercutting their normal charges. When he explained that he had taken all that the man had, he was honourably acquitted.

A client was going over a bill he had received from his lawyer. 'What's this item here?' he said. 'I don't mind paying for the lunch we had together, but what is this – "Luncheon Advice, £10"?'

'Don't you remember?' said the lawyer. 'You asked me what I recommended, and I said Beef Bourgignon.'

A young solicitor set up in practice in a small country town. For a while, business was very slow and he waited in vain for his first client. He passed the time by attending the local magistrates' court and listening to the cases; and one morning, whilst he was thus engaged, his clerk came in and whispered that there was a client waiting for him in his office. The lawyer jumped eagerly to his feet and rushed off at once. 'It's all right, sir,' his clerk shouted after him. 'He can't get away. I've locked him in.'

A very small barrister was appearing for the defence in an important trial. Before the trial opened, he encountered counsel for the prosecution outside the courtroom. Prosecuting counsel was a giant of a man and he burst out laughing when he saw his diminutive opposite number. 'So you're my opponent, are you?' he bellowed. 'Why, I could put you in my pocket!'

'If you did,' replied the tiny barrister, 'you'd have more law in your pocket than you'll ever have in your head.'

A t a crucial point in an important criminal case, the judge adjourned so that counsel for the defence could consult with his client, whose case was going very badly, and give him the benefit of his advice as to how to proceed. Half an hour later, counsel returned but there was no sign of the accused.

'Where is the accused?' asked the judge.

'He's escaped, your Honour,' said counsel. 'That was the best advice I could give him.'

An elderly barrister, as well as being very short-tempered, was also exceedingly deaf. He was appearing in a case presided over by a much younger man of whom the old silk had a very poor opinion. During the course of his very long-winded speech, the judge told him several times to wind up, and finally instructed him pointedly to sit down. As the old lawyer didn't hear a word of this, he continued speaking, upon which the judge fined him £50 for contempt of court. 'What did he say?' the barrister muttered to his clerk.

'The judge has just fined you £50 for contempt of court, sir,' the young man whispered. Glaring at the judge, the barrister reached into his pocket for his wallet and shouted, 'I'll pay it now! It's a just debt!'

Client: 'I want a divorce. My husband's been cheating on me.'

Lawyer: 'I see. Do you have any proof?'

Client: 'Yes – last night I saw him going into a cinema with another woman.'

Lawyer: 'Do you know who she was?'

Client: 'Never saw her before in my life.'

Lawyer: 'But there might be some perfectly innocent explanation. Why didn't you follow them in and find out?'
Client: 'Well, I would have done, but the chap I was with had already seen the picture.'

A doctor and a lawyer fell into conversation towards the end of a large civic dinner and reception. The doctor was in a bad mood and confided to the lawyer that he had been pestered earlier in the evening by a woman asking his advice on her medical problems. 'Why don't you send her a bill?' said the lawyer. 'After all, you rendered her professional service by giving her advice.'

'You're right,' said the doctor, 'I'll do that.' When he arrived at his surgery the following afternoon, he found a bill waiting for him from the lawyer. It read: 'For legal services – £25.'

Irish barrister: 'Your Honour, in the case before us, I maintain that it was my client's solicitor who was at fault. From evidence which has come to light, my client was not obliged to marry the young lady at all because her father had no licence for the shotgun in the first place.'

Lawyer: 'Now tell us in your own words about the fight.'
Witness: 'I never seen no fight.'
Lawyer: 'You didn't? Well tell the court just what you did see.'
Witness: 'Well, some of the lads was having a bit of a party. They started fooling around and pushing each other, and old Charlie pushed Bill Higgs a bit too hard and he fell over a table. He jumped up and pulled out a knife and took a slash at old Charlie. So then Charlie's brother, Fred, smashed a chair over Bill's head, and just then, Bill's old man rushed in with a double-barrelled shotgun and let loose both barrels into the crowd. Then Charlie's mum came rushing in from the kitchen with a carving-knife, and pretty soon the whole place was in an uproar. Well, I could see there was going to be a fight, so I got out of there as quick as I could!'

A young doctor and a young lawyer had just set up in private practice. They met in the street one day and the young doctor said, 'Great news! I've just got my first patient!'

'Congratulations!' said the young lawyer. 'When you've got him to the point where he wants to make a will, let me know and I'll go and see him.'

In outlining his case, a barrister pointed out to the court that a witness was not necessarily to be regarded as unreliable simply because he altered a statement he had previously made. 'For example,' he said, 'when I came here this morning, I would have been prepared to swear that I had my gold wristwatch with me. But I realise now that I left it at home on the bathroom shelf.'

When he got home that evening his wife said, 'I don't know why you bothered to send someone round just to collect your wristwatch.'

'I did no such thing,' said the barrister. 'You didn't give it to him, did you?'

'Of course I did,' replied his wife. 'He knew just where it was.'

A young man was up on a charge of assaulting a young lady. Owing to the nature of the case, prosecuting counsel requested that the case be heard in camera. After the court had been cleared, the young man said, 'What's this "in camera" business then?'

'Never mind about that,' prosecuting counsel snapped. 'I know what it means, the judge knows what it means, and the jury knows what it means. Continue with your evidence.'

'Well,' said the accused, 'I was walking across the common with this girl – lovely moonlit night it was – no-one about – so I thought to myself, "Now's my chance for a bit of how's-yer-father" . . .'

'Just a minute,' counsel interrupted crossly. 'What's this "how's-yer-father" business?'

'Well, I know what it means,' said the accused, 'and the judge knows what it means, and the jury knows what it means – and if you'd been there with your ruddy camera, you'd know what it means too!'

A very elderly and very deaf archbishop held a dinner party at which several notable professional men were present. At the end of the meal, as the port was being passed round, the conversation turned to the extraordinary mortality rate amongst lawyers. 'We've lost six prominent barristers in the last three weeks alone,' said a senior solicitor. At this point, the archbishop, noticing that the meal was finished and not having heard a word of the conversation, rose to say grace. 'For this and every other mercy,' he intoned, 'the Lord's name be praised!'

Lawyer: 'Now you understand that you have sworn to tell the truth, the whole truth and nothing but the truth?'
Plaintiff: 'Yes, sir.'
Lawyer: 'And you understand what will happen if you don't tell the truth?'
Plaintiff: 'Yes, sir. I'll be had up for perjury.'
Lawyer: 'Correct. And if you do tell the truth ...?'
Plaintiff: '... we lose the case!'

The plaintiff was a most attractive brunette with green eyes and an inviting smile. In summing up on her behalf, counsel for the defence said, 'Gentlemen of the jury, this young woman's fate is in your hands. What is it to be – a cold and lonely prison cell in Holloway – or her cosy little apartment at Half Moon Street, Shepherd's Market – telephone 496 6003?'

When the name of the plaintiff was called, a man in the jury-box stood up and raised his hand. 'You are the plaintiff?' said counsel for the prosecution in surprise. 'I am, sir,' the man admitted. 'Then what are you doing in the jury-box?'
'I was summoned to sit on the jury, sir.'
'Someone's evidently made a ridiculous mistake,' said counsel. 'Surely you realise that a man can't sit on the jury in his own case?'
'Well,' admitted the plaintiff, 'I thought it was a bit of luck!'

Senior silk: 'If you have the facts on your side, hammer them into the jury. If you have the law on your side, hammer it into the judge.'
Junior silk: 'But, sir, what if you have neither the facts nor the law on your side?'
Senior silk: 'Then hammer on the desk!'

Client: 'My husband is a brute and I can't stand it any more. I want to divorce him.'

Lawyer: 'Has he given you any grounds?'

Client: 'No, he hasn't.'

Lawyer: 'Well, you could let *him* divorce *you*, you know – by giving him grounds of misconduct. You know what I mean?'

Client: 'Yes – carrying on with another man. But wouldn't that be a bit expensive to arrange? I don't have any money.'

Lawyer: 'Well, in view of your financial position, I could offer you legal aid.'

Client: 'Oh, thank you very much, if you're not too busy. But it will have to be around ten o'clock on a Saturday night if he's to catch us properly.'

A lawyer was surprised one day when the door of his office opened and his local family butcher walked in. 'I'd like your advice,' said the butcher. 'If a dog came into my shop and stole some meat, would the dog's owner be obliged to pay for it?'

'Certainly,' said the lawyer. 'No question about it.'

'Well,' said the butcher, 'your dog came into my shop this morning and stole a chicken.'

'How much was it worth?' asked the lawyer.

'£5 should cover it,' replied the butcher.

'£5, eh?' said the lawyer. 'All right. My usual fee for legal advice is £30, so if you just send me a cheque for £25, we'll call it all square.'

Senior barrister giving advice to his junior: 'When you are in court, never refer to "the defendant" or "my client". Always say "Bert Smith" or "Harry Brown". Juries are quite willing to convict clients and defendants – but often they haven't the heart to convict Bert Smith or Harry Brown.'

Counsel: 'State your name please.'
Witness: 'Ethel Markham.'
Counsel: 'Are you married?'
Witness: 'Yes.'
Counsel: 'And what is your husband's occupation?'
Witness: 'He's a manufacturer.'
Counsel: 'Children?'
Witness: 'Good lord, no! Garden furniture.'

Counsel: 'Now can you positively identify my client, the accused, as the man who stole your car?'
Witness: 'Well, I could when I came in, but after your cross-examination, I'm not sure whether I ever had a car at all!'

A barrister was engaged in a long and complicated case. The presiding judge was rather elderly and found great difficulty in following some of the arguments which the barrister put forward. For his benefit, counsel went through them all again, but when he had finished, the judge said,

'I'm sorry, Mr Sherman, I regret I am none the wiser.'

'Possibly not, my lord,' replied Mr Sherman, 'but you are undoubtedly better informed.'

By a very strange coincidence, the jury selected to appear in an embezzlement case consisted entirely of ex-lawyers. The case, which was a very simple one, was duly heard, and the jury retired to consider their verdict. Hours went by and eventually the court was adjourned until half past ten the next morning. By the end of the day, however, there was still no word from the jury and the judge despatched the clerk of the court to find out what was going on. The clerk knocked on the door of the jury room and when it was opened, he asked, 'Has the jury reached a verdict?' The lawyer who had opened the door replied, 'Verdict! Certainly not! We're not yet half-way through with the nominating speeches for the foreman of the jury!'

At a trial in the Scottish Highlands, in a case concerning a motor accident, one of the witnesses was an old mountain guide. In the course of his testimony, he mentioned that he had come across the trail of a 1981 Ford Cortina. Prosecuting counsel rose to protest. 'You may be an expert on animals and the countryside,' he said, 'but are you seriously telling this court that you can determine the make and year of a car by its tracks? How did you know that it was a 1981 Ford Cortina?'

'Well, sir,' said the old man, 'I followed the trail for about a mile and found a 1981 Ford Cortina at the end of it.'

Three Scotsmen were on trial for burglary. Their arrest by a very burly police officer was being closely tested by counsel for the defence.

'Officer, you say you arrested the three men in the middle of a large car park?'

'Yes, sir.'

'What is the surface of the car park?'

'Gravel chippings, sir.'

'Did they try to run away or give any sign of hearing your approach?'

'No, sir.'

'Were you in regulation uniform at the time?'

'Yes, sir.'

'What size are your boots?'

'Eleven and a half, sir.'

'So how do you explain the failure of the accused to hear your approach?'

'I was on my bicycle at the time, sir.'

Counsel: 'Now it was at this juncture that you knocked down the plaintiff with your car?'

Witness: 'Yes – but he admitted it was his fault as he had been knocked down several times before.'

Counsel: 'I put it to you that you are not telling the truth.'

Witness: 'I do not tell lies!'

Counsel: 'Indeed? I have known you lie in this very court-room on at least two previous occasions.'

Witness: 'Ah, that's when I was guilty. I always tell the truth when I'm innocent.'

The prisoner had been truculent throughout the trial, even to the extent of dismissing his counsel. The judge was about to pass sentence but firstly asked the prisoner if he had anything to say. 'Bugger all!' muttered the prisoner.

The judge leaned over to his clerk and said, 'Did I hear the accused say something?'

'He said "bugger all", my lord,' replied the clerk.

'That's strange,' said the judge. 'I could have sworn I saw his lips move.'

A lawyer was cross-examining a witness. He asked, 'And you say you called on Mrs Jones on the 2nd of May last?'

'I object to the question,' interrupted the lawyer on the other side. There was nearly an hour's argument between the opposing counsels, and finally the judge allowed the question. 'As I was saying,' the first lawyer began again, 'on the

2nd of May, you called on Mrs Jones. Now what did she say?'

'Nothing,' replied the witness. 'She wasn't in.'

A jury in a criminal court retired to consider their verdict. They returned in an hour and asked the judge whether the prisoner had chosen his counsel himself, or whether he had been appointed by the court. The judge, puzzled, said the accused had chosen his counsel himself. The foreman then turned round and looked at the rest of the jury, all of whom nodded their heads.

'We find the prisoner insane,' he told the judge.

A judge enquired whether in fact a witness had previously been convicted. 'Yes, sir,' said the witness, 'but it was due to the incapacity of my counsel rather to any fault on my own part.'

'Yes,' said the judge with a smile. 'It always is and you have my sincere sympathy.'

'I deserve it,' replied the witness, 'seeing as you were my counsel on that occasion.'

A client received his account and thinking it was heavy, asked for an itemised breakdown. The solicitor's breakdown included the following note: 'For recognising you in the street and crossing the road to talk to you and to discuss your affairs, and re-crossing the road after discovering it was not you.'

A man charged with stealing cars was advised by his lawyer that he could be tried by a jury of his peers or by a magistrate sitting alone. 'What do you mean by peers?' asked the man. 'Peers are your equals,' said the lawyer. 'Men of your own class and kind.'

'In that case, I'll take the magistrate,' said the accused. 'I don't want to be tried by a bunch of car thieves.'

The difference between a lawyer and a surgeon is that a lawyer is always concerned with leaving nothing out and a surgeon is always concerned with leaving nothing in.

Given a man and woman staying at the same hotel, signing as Mr and Mrs, staying in the same room and sleeping in the same bed, a lawyer will always presume intimacy – unless, of course, they are husband and wife.

In a civil action, one farmer was suing his neighbour for damages for cattle trespass. The plaintiff's chief witness, a farm labourer, was in the box, being cross-examined by counsel for the defendant. 'Mr Smith – you get very strong winds in your part of the county?'

'Yes, sir.'

'Frequently, they flatten and damage standing crops?'

'Yes, sir.'

'In very much the way in which your employer's crops were damaged in this case?'

'Yes, sir.'

The counsel paused before sitting down in triumph and then asked one question too many. 'Then why did you say it was my client's cattle that were responsible?'

''Cos oi never seen the wind leave cow-muck behind, sir!'

A man, called into the jury-box at the opening of a trial, was about to take the oath when he asked to be excused, saying, 'My wife is due to conceive this afternoon and I would like to be there.' The two opposing counsels held a hurried consultation and then one of them addressed the judge. 'My lord,' he said, 'my learned friend and myself believe that the man means that his wife is about to be delivered of a child. But whether we are right, or he is right, we both certainly think he should be there.'

A fellow was driving along a country lane in a pony and trap when he was involved in a collision with a motorist. The pony and trap were overturned into a ditch. The man claimed damages and the motorist was charged. When the case came to court, counsel for the motorist rose to cross-examine the driver of the pony and trap.

Counsel: 'Is it not right that after the accident, you told the motorist that you were all right?'

Pony driver: 'That is difficult to answer.'

Counsel: 'Surely you can answer yes or no to that simple question. Tell the court what happened.'

Pony driver: 'Well, the motorist hit me and drove on. Then he stopped and came back. He saw the pony in the ditch and said, "Poor thing! Two broken legs!" Then he pulled out a gun and shot it dead. And then he turned to me and asked me if I was all right, so I said I was.'

A barrister was arguing a case before a judge who kept shaking his head in disagreement with the points the barrister was making. After this had gone on for some time, counsel turned to the jury-box and said, 'Members of the jury, you may be thinking that his Lordship's continual shaking of his head implies a difference of opinion between us, but I can assure you that when his Lordship shakes his head, there's nothing in it.'

Three little boys were caught by the vicar stealing apples from his orchard. He gave them a severe talking-to on the wickedness of stealing and then asked them what they had learned from the incident.

'Well,' said the first boy, 'my father's a doctor and I shall remember that eating stolen apples will make me sick.'

'My father is an accountant,' said the second little boy, 'and I shall remember that stealing apples is as bad as stealing money.'

'My father's a lawyer,' said the third little boy, 'and I'm going to sue you because I tore my trousers climbing down from the apple tree.'

The writer Mark Twain attended a dinner party, at the end of which he made one of his customary speeches. When it was over, a prominent lawyer got up, shoved his hands in his pockets and said, 'Doesn't it strike this company as unusual that a professional humorist should be so funny?' Everybody laughed, and then Mark Twain said, 'Doesn't it strike this company as unusual that a lawyer should have his hands in his own pockets?'

Irish judge: 'Is there any religion mixed up in this case?'
Irish barrister: 'No, my lord – both parties are Presbyterians.'

'**L**awyers earn a living by the sweat of their brow-beating.'

— **James Huneker, 1860–1921**

Lawyer: 'Now you admit that it was a very dark night and you were some way from the scene of the attack, and yet you claim that you can positively identify the defendant as the man who struck the plaintiff. Tell me this – just how far can you see at night?'
Witness: 'Well – er – how far away is the moon?'

'**W**hy do barristers wear black gowns?'
'They first started wearing them in mourning for the death of Queen Anne.'
'But why do they still wear them?'
'Well, Queen Anne's still dead, isn't she?'

Counsel: 'And what exactly was the accused doing when you arrested him?'
Arresting officer: 'He was having a violent argument with a taxi driver.'
Counsel: 'But surely that doesn't prove that he was drunk?'
Arresting officer: 'No, but there wasn't a taxi driver there.'

At the turn of the century, an old railway-crossing keeper was called as a witness in a case involving an accident between a train and a horse and cart at his crossing. Counsel subjected him to a severe cross-examination, but throughout he maintained that he had waved his lantern energetically to warn the oncoming horse and cart. He was absolved from the charge of negligence, and after the hearing counsel met him outside the courtroom and congratulated him on the way he had given his evidence.

'Thank you, sir,' said the old crossing keeper. 'But I must admit I was terribly scared that you were going to ask me whether my lantern was lit.'

A lawyer has a lot in common with a carpenter. For instance, a lawyer can file an affidavit, chop logic, frame an indictment, bore a court and chisel a client.

Solicitor: 'Are you able to pay anything at all towards the costs of the case?'
Client: 'No. I've already turned over everything I have to the judge and two of the jury.'

Two barristers almost came to blows during an action in which they were engaged on opposing sides. One of them declared that when the case was over, he would tell his opponent exactly what he thought of him. When they met outside the courtroom, the first barrister said, 'You're a rogue, sir! Is there any cause so bad that you wouldn't support it, or any villain that you wouldn't defend if the fee was big enough?'

'I don't know,' said his opponent. 'What have you been doing?'

Abraham Lincoln was a great lawyer and also a great humanitarian. A man once came and asked him to help him prosecute a neighbour who owed him $2.50. Knowing that the neighbour was very poor, Lincoln agreed to take the case and asked for $10 as his legal fee. He then gave $5 to the impoverished neighbour, who promptly settled the debt and ended up in pocket.

'Now, Miss Smith,' said counsel, 'will you please tell the court exactly what the young man said to you.'

'Oh, I couldn't do that!' said the witness, blushing furiously. 'It was very rude!'

'All right,' said counsel, 'just write down what he said and I'll pass it round the jury.' Miss Smith complied and handed the slip of paper to the lawyer. He glanced at what she had written and gasped. 'Do you mean to say that the defendant

actually asked you this?' he said. 'Yes, he did.' 'I see! Bailiff, pass this paper among the jury.'

The bailiff handed the note to the foreman of the jury who blinked several times and passed it to the next juror. And so it went on round the jurymen, each one flushing, turning pale or gasping in disbelief. The note reached the last juror who had been fast asleep throughout the whole incident. His neighbour nudged him and passing him the note, whispered, 'From the girl in the witness box.' The juror read the note, glanced at the witness, and then smiled contentedly and put the paper in his pocket.

Accused: 'Your Honour, my lawyer is ill and I would like to have my case postponed until next week.'

Judge: 'What for? You were arrested in the very act of stealing the plaintiff's wallet. What can your lawyer possibly say in your defence?'

Accused: 'That's what I want to find out!'

'Brown is certainly a smart fellow. He's drawn up his will in such a way that his lawyer won't be able to get more out of it than the beneficiaries.'

'How did he manage that?'

'He's left half his estate to the lawyer, provided he sees to it that the beneficiaries get the other half.'

A rich farmer approached a lawyer with a view to enlisting his services in a lawsuit. The lawyer informed him that he had already been engaged by the other side but promised to give him a recommendation to another lawyer. When he got home, the farmer opened the letter out of curiosity. It read: 'Here are two fat wethers, fallen out together; if you'll fleece one, I'll fleece the other, and make them agree like brother and brother.'

A young lawyer appearing in court for the first time allowed his enthusiasm to run away with him. As he addressed the court, he soared higher and higher on the wings of eloquence. Finally, the judge stopped him and said, 'Please don't go any higher – you are already out of the jurisdiction of this court.'

Lawyer: 'Now is it not the case that on the 5th of November last, you rode naked through the streets on top of a dustcart, letting off fireworks, waving a pair of pants and singing *I Did It My Way* at the top of your voice?'
Witness: 'What was the date again?'

Irish barrister: 'You are claiming compensation from your employers for injuries sustained when you were struck on the head by a falling hammer. However, I have to advise you that since you were not wearing a safety helmet at the time, you haven't a leg to stand on!'

A visitor to Scotland saw a funeral procession. He asked who the deceased was, and on learning that it was a local lawyer, asked, 'Do you bury lawyers in Scotland, then?'

'Aye, we do,' he was told. 'What do you do with them in England?'

'Well, when they die, we just put them in a room, close the door and leave them there overnight. In the morning, they're gone.'

'That's very strange. Is there no sign of their going?'

'Nothing except a strong smell of brimstone.'

A man was accused of stealing a pig. He engaged a rather shady lawyer to defend him. 'Have you still got the carcass?' asked the lawyer.

'Yes, I have.'

'Then I want you to go home, cut the pig lengthwise, keep one half and give me the other.'

When the trial came, the lawyer rose to his feet and said, 'My lord, the accused has no more of that stolen pig than I have myself.' The prisoner was acquitted.

'**I** don't think you've appeared before me in the past, Mr Berry?' said the judge, addressing a young barrister. 'No, my lord. But the name is Bewry.'

'How do you spell that?' asked the judge.

'B-U-R-Y, my lord.'

'Well, that's pronounced Berry,' said the judge rather crossly. 'You may proceed, Mr Berry.'

'Thank you, my lord,' said the barrister. He was only a little way into his speech, however, when he collapsed with laughter and was unable to continue. 'What on earth is the matter with you?' asked the judge.

'I'm sorry, my lord,' gasped the barrister, the tears rolling down his cheeks. 'It's just that a thought has suddenly struck me. Those twelve people sitting over there think they're serving on a jury – but we know better, don't we, my lord?'

A man was accused of stealing £1000 so he hired a lawyer to defend him. 'Now first of all,' said the lawyer, 'I must know whether or not you did steal the money.'

'Yes, I did,' admitted the man.

'And how much of it have you got left?'

'About £50,' said the client.

'Well, then, you'd better stand trial and take your chances.'

'I suppose I'll have to,' said the man. 'How much do I owe you for that advice?'

'£50,' replied the lawyer.

A lawyer appearing for the wife in a marital case in which both sides claimed custody of the child, took the little boy in his arms and showed him to the jury with tears running down the youngster's cheeks. His opponent, appearing for the husband, called the little boy up and asked him, 'Why were you crying just now?'

'Because,' replied the little lad, 'that man pinched me!'

Irish barrister: 'You don't seem to understand the seriousness of your situation. Do you realise where you are?'
Irish witness: 'Yes, sir, I do. This is a court of law.'
Irish barrister: 'And do you know what that is?'
Irish witness: 'Yes, sir – it's a place where they dispense with justice.'

A defence witness in a murder trial alleged that the accused had only been absent from a party for a matter of three or four minutes and could not possibly have committed a murder in such a short space of time. Prosecuting counsel turned to the jury and said, 'Gentlemen, observe the clock on the wall. I shall pause now for a period of three minutes and you may consider what could have been done by the accused in that period.' As the 180 seconds ticked by, the wait seemed interminable. The jury returned a verdict of guilty.

A man who fell through an open manhole sued the city council for damages after sustaining a broken leg. He engaged a lawyer to act for him and won the case. After the claim was settled, the lawyer sent for his client and handed him a £5 note. 'What's this?' asked the litigant.

'That's your damages,' replied the lawyer, 'after deducting the cost of the case and my expenses.'

The man turned the £5 note over and carefully examined both sides. 'What's the matter with this note?' he asked. 'Is it counterfeit?'

A prominent barrister was featured in a big court case and became very well known as a result. Having to undertake a journey up north, he went along to the station and bought a ticket. In examining his change, he found that he had been given £5 too much. Accordingly, he returned to the ticket office, pointed out the mistake and handed back the £5. 'Well!' said the ticket clerk in surprise, 'and you a lawyer too!'

It is not uncommon to hear prisoners express dissatisfaction with their counsel, but on one occasion, a prisoner, having pleaded guilty, listened with great admiration to his defence lawyer, and when he had finished, asked to change his plea as he was now convinced of his own innocence.

Barristers have always been very clever at leading witnesses into a trap. A witness at a murder trial attested that a hat which was produced in evidence had fallen from the head of the murderer as he was running away from the scene of the crime. With the hat in his hand, counsel for the defence said, 'You saw this hat fall from the prisoner's head?'

'Yes, sir, I did.'

'So you picked it up?'

'Yes, sir.'

'And I suppose you examined it, outside and in?'

'Yes.'

Counsel glanced inside the hat, and appearing to read from the label, said, 'And I suppose you read the name of the accused, O'Connell, on the lining?'

'Yes, sir,' replied the witness immediately.

'My lord,' said counsel, 'I request that the charges be withdrawn against my client. There is no name in the hat.'

One of the most prominent 19th-century American lawyers was walking through town one day when he noticed a sale going on of the effects of a poor widow whose house was being sold up. The item being sold at that moment was a sugar bowl and the poor widow said to the purchaser, 'I'll just take the sugar out before you go.' The purchaser protested that he had bought the bowl complete with its contents, and a violent argument ensued. Noticing the lawyer, the buyer appealed to him about the rights of the

case. The lawyer considered for a moment and then agreed that the sale of the sugar bowl undoubtedly included its contents. But just as the miserly purchaser turned to go, he added, 'Just a minute. My fee for legal advice is $100. Unless you pay me on the spot, I shall sue you for the full amount.' The purchaser realised that he had been caught and paid up at once, whereupon the lawyer handed over the money to the poor old widow.

A famous Irish advocate, O'Connell, was standing outside the Dublin courthouse one day when a lady approached him and asked him to direct her to an honest lawyer. O'Connell scratched his head and said, 'Well, now, you beat me entirely, ma'am.'

Client: 'I want to thank you for defending me so success-fully in court. How much do I owe you?'
Lawyer: 'Well, seeing that your father and I were old friends, we'll say £200.'
Client: '£200! Thank heavens you didn't know my grand-father as well!'

'A man may as well open an oyster without a knife as a lawyer's mouth without a fee.'
— Barten Holyday, 1593–1661

A woman seeking a divorce went to visit her solicitor. The first question he asked her was, 'Do you have grounds?'

'Yes,' she replied, 'about four acres.'

'Perhaps I'm not making myself clear,' he said. 'Do you have a grudge?'

'No, but we have a parking space,' she responded.

'Can I put it another way. Does your husband beat you up?' he said impatiently.

'No, generally I get up before he does.'

By this stage the solicitor decided to try a different tack. 'Are you sure you really want a divorce?' he said.

'I don't want one at all,' she replied, 'but my husband does. He claims we have difficulty communicating.'